Thirty Reflective Devotions for Time-Pressed Women

Greater Intimacy with your Heavenly Father

JOY FRY

WESTBOW
P R E S S
A DIVISION OF THOMAS NELSON

WestBow Press books may be ordered through
booksellers or by contacting:

WestBow Press
A Division of Thomas Nelson
1663 Liberty Drive
Bloomington, IN 47403
www.westbowpress.com
1-(866) 928-1240

NIV – New International Version
Scripture taken from the Holy Bible, New International
Version®. Copyright © 1973, 1978, 1984 Biblica. Used
by permission of Zondervan. All rights reserved.

ISBN: 978-1-4497-7881-1 (e)
ISBN: 978-1-4497-7880-4 (sc)

Library of Congress Control Number: 2012923306

Printed in the United States of America

WestBow Press rev. date: 12/19/2012

CONTENTS

DEDICATION

This book is dedicated to my friend Carolyn for her faith and courage while she was undergoing many months of cancer treatments. She allowed me to experience the journey with her. She shared her struggles, pain, and thoughts during the treatments. I am filled with thankfulness for the Lord's strength and comfort provided to Carolyn during this difficult season of her life.

An Introduction

This book comes out of my desire for others to experience a daily walk with God in which He speaks through His Word and the Holy Spirit during times of quiet reflection. Each devotion in the book is designed to take 15 minutes although you may want to spend more time on days that your schedule allows.

I struggled for many years to make a daily devotion part of my schedule-packed day. For me, what works best is to have my devotional time first thing in the morning (with coffee but before any other activities). I use a format of reading the devotion, then journaling, and praying. It is my hope that reading this book would be the beginning of a greater desire to spend time (even 15 minutes a day) having your spirit nourished through personal time alone with God.

Also, I trust that this book will provide a foundation for you to grow in the knowledge that you have a God and Father who knows you intimately. He is by your side today and for the road ahead and into eternity.

Here are several suggestions for how to get started with this book:

- Find a quiet place and time you can read and write

- Begin with prayer; Ask God to still your mind
- Have a Bible and a journal nearby to respond to the daily reflections.

Also, here are some ideas for using this book:

- Read the devotions in the order listed or in any order
- Take time to reflect, journal, or pray in response to the Bible verse or devotion
- Meditate on or memorize the Bible verse
- Write your own response or use the questions provided to respond to the verses, poems and reflective writings

The poetic meditations were written over several years. I participated and then led Christian women writers groups. The format of the writers' group was that a scripture verse was read and then I wrote in response to the scripture. The scripture was the inspiration for the poems in this devotion.

The wildflower photos on the book covers were taken in Central California by Ray R. Morawski.

SECTION 1:
FRUIT OF THE SPIRIT

DAY 1

GIFTS OF THE FATHER

Bible Reading: Romans 6:23

For the wages of sin is death, but the gift of God is eternal life in Christ Jesus our Lord.

As believers we can rest in the promise of God's Word that our sins are forgiven and we have eternal life. We can continually express our thankfulness to God for the gifts of grace, communion, and the Holy Spirit.

Poem

His Word is true,
It was written for me and you.

His Son provides grace,
It was He who died for our sins and evil ways.

His baptism replenishes our soul,
It washes us clean and makes us whole.

His body and blood we eat and drink,

He forgives our sins, in spite of what others think.

His Spirit is alive in those who believe,
He was given to provide guidance and to lead.
Amen.

Prayer Response

Heavenly Father,
My heart is full of thanksgiving for your gifts. I praise you for forgiving my sins through the precious blood of your Son. May I not take these gifts for granted.

Amen.

For Reflection

- Visualize that you are in Jesus's presence.
- Share any specific sins on your heart with Him and let His forgiveness and love wash over you.
- Write a prayer of thanksgiving and confession.

DAY 2

JOY

Bible Reading: Nehemiah 8:10

Nehemiah said, "Go and enjoy choice food and sweet drinks, and send some to those who have nothing prepared. This day is sacred to the Lord. Do not grieve, for the joy of the Lord is your strength."

This verse reminded me of two things. First, we can find joy from sharing with the poor, and with those who are physically or mentally disabled. Second, when we celebrate and proclaim God's goodness, He will provide us with strength.

Prayer Response

Dear Father,

You are my song who gives joy to my heart and lips. I will praise you. I will praise you. I will praise you. Alleluia. Alleluia. Alleluia. Amen.

For Reflection

- What acts of service for God bring you joy?

- How has the Lord provided you with strength to serve others?

DAY 3

LOVING ONE ANOTHER

Bible Reading: Luke 10:30-37-The Parable of the Good Samaritan

"A man was going down from Jerusalem to Jericho when he fell into the hands of robbers. They stripped him of his clothes, beat him and went away, leaving him half dead. A priest happened to be going down the same road, and when he saw the man, he passed by on the other side. So too a Levite, when he came to the place and saw him, passed by on the other side. But a Samaritan, as he traveled came where the man was and when he saw him, he took pity on him. He went to him and bandaged his wounds, pouring on oil and wine. Then he put the man on his own donkey, took him to an inn and took care of him. The next day he took out two silver coins and gave them to the innkeeper. Look after him, he said, and when I return, I will reimburse you for any extra expense you may have.' "Which of these do you think was a neighbor to the man who fell into the hands of

robbers?" The expert in the law replied, "The one who had mercy on him."

In this parable we are reminded of the Lord's desire for us to serve others. We are called to love and serve when the needs of others arise. We may have to help when it is inconvenient or when there is no earthly gain for us. Thankfully, our God and Father will provide us with strength and compassion when we call upon Him rather than trying to "help out" on our own strength.

Poem

> Show mercy to those in need
> Don't count the cost of the deed
>
> Give freely when a stranger needs your help this day
> Rather than ignoring the problem which is in your way
>
> Avoid the tendency to judge another's woe
> Instead, try to help with lightening their load
>
> Allow your acts of love
> To flow from strength from above

Prayer Response

Heavenly Father,

Will you teach me to demonstrate love to others as the Samaritan did in this Parable? I need your help to love difficult people. Thank you for sending your Son to mankind as the ultimate act of love. Amen.

For Reflection

- Do we leave loving for others to do?
- Do we show love only to those who love us?
- Do we love to impress others or to satisfy our own agenda?

DAY 4

GOD'S LOVING KINDNESS

Bible Reading: Jeremiah 31:3

The Lord appeared to us in the past, saying: "I have loved you with an everlasting love; I have drawn you with loving kindness."

We can rest in the promise of these words. Our loving Father has promised us a love that will not end no matter how many times we fail or make mistakes. Instead, He continually calls us back to Him with tenderness and patience.

Prayer Response

Father,

Thank you that we can have an eternal and loving relationship with you when we put our faith and trust in you. Alleluia. Glory in the Highest. Amen.

For Reflection

- How has God shown you His loving kindness?

- Close your eyes and think of your heavenly Father wrapping His arms of love around you.
- Write a response to God for his loving kindness.

DAY 5

PERFECT PEACE

Bible Reading: John 14:25-27

"All this I have spoken while still with you. But, the Counselor, the Holy Spirit, whom the Father will send in my name, will teach you all things and will remind you of everything I have said to you. Peace I leave with you; my peace I give to you. I do not give to you as the world gives. Do not let your hearts be troubled and do not be afraid. "

What comfort we can experience when we allow the Holy Spirit into our life. We can exchange our anxieties and fears for peace in our spirit. During times of troubles and trials, we are promised we can still have peace.

Prayer Response

Oh Lord,

What a mystery it is to me that you are the peace giver in all circumstances. I thank you for the gift of the Holy Spirit to provide me with comfort and peace. May I seek you first in times of trouble and when I feel anxious or afraid. Amen.

For Reflection

- What daily experiences cause you to become fearful or anxious?
- Write a letter to God telling Him about your fears and asking for Him to provide His perfect peace.

SECTION 2:
TRIUMPH OVER
EARTHLY TROUBLES

DAY 6

BURDENS LIFTED

Bible Reading: Psalm 68:19

Praise be to the Lord, to God our Savior, who daily bears our burdens.

Many of us begin this day bearing burdens. We or someone we love may be experiencing one or more of the following: anxiety, fear, depression, pain, loss, sadness, or loneliness. These burdens all weigh heavily on our heart and mind. May we hold fast to the promise that God, our Father, wants to carry these burdens for us as we surrender them to Him.

Poem

Lay your burdens upon my shoulders, says the Lord.
Place them upon me and let them go.
Let me carry the things causing pain.
Don't hold on or try to seize them back.

I can bare your sorrow and pain.
You have carried them long enough.

It is time to release them and focus on me.
I am the author and the perfector of your faith.

Go in my peace today.
Knowing that your burdens are lifted.
Your heavy heart has been set free.
A gift from me.

Prayer Response

Dear Father,
Thank you for bearing each of my burdens. Will you give me the humility to release each one to you and trust your plan? Amen.

For Reflection

- Take a moment to identify and write down any specific burdens you are carrying.
- Spend some time in prayer releasing the burdens to the Lord. Let Him take them and comfort you.

DAY 7

POWER OVER FEAR

Bible Reading: II Timothy 1:7

For God did not give a spirit of timidity, but a spirit of power, of love, and of self-discipline.

How encouraging to know we don't need to become paralyzed with fear when unexpected events and circumstances arise. We can claim the Lord's promises to give us the power and victory to overcome our fears and doubts.

Prayer Response

Dear Father,

Thank you for your Word. As we obey your Word and display the spiritual gifts you provide, may we hold on to your promise to receive power and not fear. May we take steps forward in faith without stopping to look towards the right or left. Amen.

For Reflection

- Take a few minutes to write down the areas where you are experiencing fear in stepping out in faith.
- Write your own prayer asking for the Father's strength and power.

DAY 8

SEASON OF SORROW

Bible Reading: Nehemiah 8:10

Nehemiah said, "Go and enjoy choice food and sweet drinks, and send some to those who have nothing prepared. This day is sacred to the Lord. Do not grieve, for the joy of the Lord is your strength."

God promises that even in times of earthly sorrow and pain, He can supply us with joy. This may be difficult to grasp but we have the promise from God that He can fill our spirit with joy and strength even while our earthly body is suffering physical or emotional pain.

Prayer Response

Dear Father,

I adore you. May my heart be holy and humble before you. Help me to release any pain I feel within. And, to remember you died for my sin. In all things, may I rest in your plan, remembering

you will guide me and we will walk hand in hand.
Alleluia. Amen.

For Reflection

- Write down any areas of your life in which you desire joy despite your circumstances.
- Remember a time when the Lord provided you with strength during a time of trials.

DAY 9

FACING TRIALS

Bible Reading: John 16:33

"I have told you these things, so that in me you may have peace. In this world you will have trouble. But take heart! I have overcome the world."

God has not promised that our earthly life will be easy or pain free. If we can accept that we will experience trouble in our daily life experiences, then we don't need to run from it or try to understand the pain and suffering. Rather, we can ask our heavenly Father to bear our burdens and to provide peace and endurance during the trials.

Prayer Response

Dear Father,

May I remember that joy will abound without a sound, as I release my cares to you. Thank you for providing me with strength and peace in the midst of my current circumstances. Amen.

For Reflection

- What trials are you experiencing for which you desire God's peace?
- Close your eyes and reflect on how you would feel if God's peace were to fill you.

DAY 10

FREEDOM FROM
EARTHLY FEARS

Bible Reading: Psalm 34:4,7

I sought the Lord, and he answered me; he delivered me from all my fears. The angel of the Lord encamps around those who fear him, and he delivers them.

Prayer Response

Dear Father,

You have delivered us from our earthly fears. We don't have to hide when we struggle with the trials of this earthly life. Instead, we can call upon your name. We can ask for deliverance from the paralysis of indecision and inaction. We can cry out in times of weakness and confusion. We can claim your Word as the guiding light when we are stuck in a state of darkness. We can ask you to fill us with the counsel and the comfort of the Holy Spirit. Thank you that you conquer each of our fears and are victorious in each earthly struggle we face. Alleluia. Glory in the Highest. Amen.

For Reflection

- What fears are gripping you?
- Spend some time with your eyes closed and visualize releasing over to God each of these fears and claiming His victory over them.

DAY 11

OVERCOMING TEMPTATION

Bible Reading: James 1:13-14

When tempted, no one should say, "God is tempting me." For God cannot be tempted by evil, nor does he tempt anyone; but each one is tempted when, by his own evil desire, he is dragged away and enticed.

We face temptations every day for we live in a world filled with sin. If we don't recognize and accept temptation, we will face it regularly. Then we may be caught off guard when temptations arise. Temptations can come in the form of thoughts, words, or actions. Temptations can torment. How encouraging to know that God is not the source of our temptations. We can claim victory over temptation by His Word and promises to overcome evil.

Prayer Response

Father,

I come before you and ask for protection from the temptation and allure of sin. May I remember to call upon your name during each time of weakness

and ask for victory over the enemy. Alleluia. Glory
to your name. Amen.

For Reflection

- Write down any temptations you are
  facing.
- Also, reflect on what steps you will take
  to protect yourself from temptations.

DAY 12

LET'S SING PRAISES

Bible Reading: Psalm 103:1-2

Praise the Lord, O my soul; all my innermost being, praise his holy name. Praise the Lord, O my soul, and forget not all his benefits.

These words remind us that God longs for us to praise Him and to remember all the ways He provides for us. We can practice praise in the face of any circumstance. This discipline of praising can bring joy and peace to us. We are promised His goodness when we worship the Lord and acknowledge His faithfulness.

Prayer Response

Dear Father,

I confess praising your name can be difficult some days. And yet I know that when I do praise your name, my spirit is lifted and my heart is less heavy. Thank you for the gift of praise. Amen.

For Reflection

- What are the ways you practice praising God (singing, worship, writing, praying)?
- Take some time to praise him now.

DAY 13

RENEWED HOPE

Bible Reading: Isaiah 40:31

But those who hope in the Lord will renew their strength. They will soar on wings like eagles; they will run and not grow weary, and they will walk and not be faint.

When we, as believers, face various trials, including loss, pain, and unfulfilled dreams, we can call upon the Lord for strength to endure the journey. We can ask that our hope be restored moment by moment in all areas of our life. What a joy to know that we do not walk alone during difficult seasons of our life.

Prayer Response

Dear Father,

Thank you for providing me with strength when the load of this earthly life feels like too much to endure. Thank you that I can call upon you as my refuge and strength. Alleluia. Glory in the highest. Amen.

For Reflection

- In what areas of your life do you desire your hope to be renewed or restored?
- Write a letter or prayer asking God to restore that hope.

SECTION 3:
THE CHARACTER
OF JESUS

DAY 14

OBEDIENCE

Bible Reading: Luke 14:1-4

One Sabbath, when Jesus went to eat at the house of a prominent Pharisee, he was being carefully watched. There in front of him was a man suffering from dropsy. Jesus asked the Pharisees and experts in the law, "Is it lawful to heal on the Sabbath or not" But they remained silent. So taking hold of the man, he healed him and sent him away.

We can ask our Heavenly Father to provide us with the power and strength to remain obedient to His Word and to His plan.

Poem

Oh, the healing power of Jesus' hand,
Destined to be used throughout the land.

In spite of judgment from people of His time,
Jesus obeyed his Father's command to step over
the Pharisee's line.

When His eyes gazed on those in need,
He did not hesitate to help regardless of the
reaction to His deed.

Jesus showed compassion to those suffering
and in pain,
He even healed those who for many years had
been lame.

May we too be faithful to God's will,
Even when the influence of others tempts us to
be still. Amen.

Prayer Response

Dear Father,

Will you give me the power to be obedient to
your Word and the guidance of the Holy Spirit
when I am called to serve others? Alleluia. Amen.

For Reflection

- How can I remain steadfast to the things
  I feel called to do, in spite of what others
  think?
- Will I step out in obedience and faith
  in spite of the potential risks to my
  reputation and relationships?
- Where are you calling me to step out and
  serve others in need?

DAY 15

HIS LIGHT

Bible Reading; Matthew 5:16

In the same way, let your light shine before men, that they may see your good deeds and praise your Father in heaven.

Regardless of our present circumstances, the light of the Lord can shine through our lives by our words and actions toward others. Let us remember to ask our God and Father to whom He intends for us to show light and love this day.

The Lord is the light of our life, giving us guidance and leading us out of darkness and sin. We are called to live as children of the light and to radiate his light forever. We are to be a lantern always shining with the love of Christ and displaying the light that is goodness, truth, and righteousness. May our words and actions reflect the Lord's light.

Prayer Response

Holy Father,
    Will you shine your light upon me,
    For others to be drawn to see?

    May I glow with your Spirit of love,
    And focus on things above.

    In all my words and deeds this day,
    I long to hear what you have to say. Alleluia.
Amen.

For Reflection

- With whom do you think God is calling you to share your light?
- Where are you called to be a light of faith?

DAY 16

SURRENDER

Bible Reading: Psalm 40:8

I desire to do your will, O my God; your law is within my heart.

We may face struggles in relinquishing control to God in many areas of our daily lives including relationships, finances, and time commitments. We may surrender control and then find we want to take control again. To let go takes trust and faith in a loving God and Father.

Poem

There is joy in surrender to the Holy One.
There is peace in the presence of the Holy One.
There is guidance from the Spirit of the Holy One.
There is everlasting love from the Holy One.
O, God and Father, I surrender all to you.

Prayer Response

Dear Heavenly Father,

I confess how difficult I find it to surrender some areas of my life to you and trust your perfect plan. I long for you to be my leader and guide. Alleluia. Amen.

For Reflection

- What part of my life do I desire to surrender more to you, oh, Holy One?
- What are the fears that keep me from surrendering more to you?

DAY 17

SERVING OTHERS

Bible Reading: Matthew 14:23,35-36

After he had dismissed them, he went up on a mountain side by himself to pray. And when the men of that place recognized Jesus, they sent word to all the surrounding country. People brought all their sick to him and begged him to let the sick just touch the edge of his cloak, and all who touched him were healed.

The Lord delights in having us spend time alone with Him whether reading His Word or spending time in prayer. In addition, He uses this time to refresh and renew us so we can spend time serving others. Prayer includes both talking with God and listening to the guidance of the Holy Spirit.

Poem

Go and make believers of all.
The disciples heard his call.

Model Jesus's time spent alone and in prayer,

Be the one to stop for the sick and provide care.

Reach out to the Savior who is near,
Ask him to calm your mind filled with doubt
and fear.

Expect challenges as you serve the Lord each day,
Don't be distracted by what others think and say.

Hold fast to the promises of the Word,
And, the teachings of Jesus you have heard.

Prayer Response

Heavenly Father,
I confess at times I am tempted not to set aside time with you. Will you provide the strength and discipline for me to spend time in your Word each day? Will you use this time to show me where you are calling me to serve and love others? Amen.

For Reflection

- Identify the time each day that you will set aside to spend alone with Jesus.
- What do you find most difficult about spending time alone with Jesus?
- Ask God where He is calling you to serve in the coming days and weeks. Is it in your church body, family, neighborhood, or somewhere else?

DAY 18

WORDS OF TRUTH

Bible Reading: Isaiah 45:19

I have not spoken in secret, from somewhere in a land of darkness; I have not said to Jacob's descendants, seek me in vain. I, the Lord, speak the truth; I declare what is right.

As we face choices in our daily life, we can trust the guidance of the Lord's Word. We can take time to read His promises and call upon Him in prayer.

Prayer Response

Dear Father,

I glorify your name. Your Word is a safe place to calm my heart and mind in times of fear, anxiety, and pain. I cling to your promises and your words of truth. Your spirit convicts me of my sin, weaknesses, and insecurities. I ask for daily guidance as the choices and the decisions weighing on my heart can feel overwhelming. Alleluia. Glory in the highest. Amen.

For Reflection

- What choices do I face in which I desire the guidance of the Word?
- In which areas of my life do I desire to cling to promises in the Word?

DAY 19

SEEKING GOD'S WILL

Bible Reading: Psalm 40:4,8

Blessed is the man who makes the Lord his trust, who does not look to the proud, to those who turn aside to false Gods. "I desire to do your will, O my God; your law is within my heart."

We, as believers, know the Lord desires our obedience. And yet, we often struggle to trust the Lord when worldly temptations arise and distract us. Thankfully, the Lord is patient as we grow to trust Him more.

Prayer Response

Oh Lord,

I desire to do your will, and not to give in to temptation or seek what I see others enjoying.
You instruct me not to be enticed by false gods.
Your law is in my heart to guide me and protect me when I seek your will.
You hear my cry when I feel discouraged and need my hope restored.

You promise blessings when I put my trust in you.
You pull me out of my despair when I experience loss, sadness or pain.
You offer mercy, love, and the restoration of hope.
You plant my feet on the solid foundation of your eternal love.
You have created all that my eyes gaze upon.
You ask me to wait patiently for your perfect will to be done.

Alleluia. Amen.

For Reflection

- In what areas of your life are you waiting for God's will to be revealed?
- In what areas do you want to give up "your will" and seek "His will"?

DAY 20

FAITHFUL SERVANT

Bible Reading: Matthew 25:21

"His master replied, 'Well done, good and faithful servant! You have been faithful with a few things; I will put you in charge of many things. Come and share your master's happiness!'

This verse encourages us to remain faithful, expecting that the Lord will honor our obedience by providing us with even more opportunities to serve him. What a joy that we can use the gifts He has given us to provide for others, serving them with prayer, hospitality, or teaching.

Prayer Response

Dear Father,

I ask you to increase my faith so I can obey and serve you faithfully. Alleluia. Amen.

For Reflection

- Where do you feel gifted to serve others?

- Have you experienced joy by using your gifts? Describe your experience.

SECTION 4: PROMISES

DAY 21

OUR GUIDE

Bible Reading: Isaiah 42:16

I will lead the blind by ways they have not known, along unfamiliar paths I will guide them; I will turn the darkness into light before them and make the rough places smooth. These are the things I will do; I will not forsake them.

O Lord, you are our steadfast guide when we face choices along life's path. You hold us close and provide your Word, your Spirit and fellow believers to guide and lead us. We need not face decisions alone.

Poem

Oh Lord, it is you I want to trust,
Out of my love, and not because I must.

How great is your promise to be our guide,
May I not rely on ways that others have tried.

Your steadfastness is good and true,

May I ever hold fast to words from you.

Thank you for soothing my inner confusion and fear,
And, holding me near. Amen.

Prayer Response

Father,
    I give thanks that you can soothe my inner fears
and confusion just like warm oil covering all aches
inside my heart. I ask for strength to trust the plan
you have designed for me. Amen.

For Reflection

- Write a response to the verse or poetic reflection expressing any thoughts or feelings you had from reading them.
- Identify any areas of your life where you desire God's guidance in upcoming decisions.

DAY 22

OUR HOPE

Bible Reading: Psalm 33:20-22

We wait in hope for our Lord; he is our help and our shield. In him our hearts rejoice, for we trust in his holy name. May your unfailing love rest upon us, O Lord, even as we put our hope in you.

Whether experiencing times of joy or sorrow, how reassuring to know we can put our hope in the Lord. We need not seek our future security or plans from any source other than the Lord.

Prayer Response

Dear Father,

I thank you that I can put my hope in you. I can call upon you when I need help and I am promised your unfailing love. I can ask for a willingness to fear you and not fear the power and strength of those who do not believe in your name. May I walk in the knowledge of your help and protection all of my days, both now and in eternity. To Him are all honor, glory and praise, forever and ever. Amen.

For Reflection

- In what areas of your life do you need your hope restored?
- How has God restored your hope when you have faced difficult circumstances in the past?

DAY 23

OUR REFUGE

Bible Reading: Psalm 36:5-7

Your love, O Lord, reaches to the heavens, your faithfulness to the skies. Your righteousness is like the mighty mountains, your justice like the great deep. O Lord, you preserve both man and beast. How priceless is your unfailing love. Both high and low among men find refuge in the shadow of your wings.

These words remind us we can rest under the care of God's perfect will. We can find strength through quiet times of reflecting on His Word. We can cry out to God in our despair and trust He will provide comfort for us. We can speak to God in prayer and ask for His perfect will to be done. We can trust that God will provide times of rest and restoration for our mind, soul, and body. We can hold fast to God's promises when trials surround us. We can call upon fellow believers to sit with us in our times of need.

Prayer Response

Dear Father,

Thank you for being the provider who can fulfill our spiritual, emotional and physical needs. Alleluia. Glory in the highest. Amen.

For Reflection

- Write a note to God or a prayer thanking him for his faithfulness in your life.
- Reflect on any areas where you desire the Lord's will to be done through you.

DAY 24

THE MIRACLE OF GRACE

Bible Reading: I Timothy 2:5

For there is one God and one mediator between God and men, the man Jesus Christ, who gave himself as a ransom for all men-the testimony given in its proper time.

May we reflect today on the miraculous birth, death, and resurrection of our Lord, Jesus Christ. To Him we give honor, glory, and praise, forever and ever. Amen.

Poem

The Journey

His face was worn and wrinkled,
Signs of nights without sleep and days with little food

His body was exhausted,
Signs of three years of traveling and often speaking to large groups

His skin was tanned and ruddy,
Signs of hours spent riding on a donkey or walking from city to city

His eyes were bright and full of light,
Signs of the fullness of glory bestowed from His Father

His soul was sorrow filled and troubled,
Signs of the pain which lay ahead in the days to come

His head was too heavy to keep upright,
Signs of hanging on the cross for too long

His spirit was uplifted when he was resurrected,
A sign that His promise for becoming man had been fulfilled

Prayer Response

Dear Father,
What a loving God you are. May I hold fast to remembering the birth, death and resurrection of your Son each day. May I never take the gift of grace for granted. Amen.

For Reflection

- Meditate on the gift of God's grace for all your sins.
- Write a prayer of thanksgiving to your Lord and Savior.

DAY 25

THE LORD'S DIVINE WILL

Bible Reading: Matthew 6:9-13

"This, then, is how you ought to pray:" 'Our Father in heaven, hallowed be your name, Your kingdom come, your will be done on earth as it is in heaven. Give us today our daily bread. Forgive us our debts, as we also have forgiven our debtors. And lead us not into temptation but deliver us from the evil one.'

Oh, how we struggle with the Father's will and not "ours" to be done. May we trust and surrender more to His divine leading. May we release our agenda for relationships, time, and finances. May we remember God's promises to love us and provide for us as His children.

Prayer Response

Dear Father,

Thank you for showing us in this prayer how we are to pray. May I trust in your perfect plan for my life. Amen.

For Reflection

- How would your day be the same or different if doing God's will was your primary focus?
- Is there something God is calling you to give up? What do you need more of?

DAY 26

NEW BEGINNINGS

Bible Reading: Song of Solomon 2:11-12

See! The winter is past; the rains are over and gone. Flowers appear on the earth;

Do you need a new beginning? A fresh start freed from past failures and mistakes. God offers that promise of a new start if we ask for forgiveness and repent over the behavior. He will provide a clean slate for us to begin again without guilt or fear.

Prayer Response

Dear Father,

Thank you for giving me a new beginning when I have sinned and not obeyed you. Free me from guilt and allow me to wait expectantly for your plan to unfold. Amen.

For Reflection

- Take a moment and write down any areas of your life where you desire a new beginning.

- Write a prayer to God confessing your need for a new beginning.

DAY 27

CHILDREN OF GOD

Bible Reading: Ephesians 1:4

For he chose us in him before the creation of the world to be holy and blameless in his sight.

As children of the Father we are promised the gift of grace and of a personal relationship with God through Jesus Christ. As we submit to the Holy Spirit's guidance, our lives can reflect the Lord's holiness and light. We can rest on the promise that our sins have been forgiven and we can reach out to God without guilt or shame.

Prayer Response

Dear Father,

May I hold fast to your promise that I am your child. May I remember that you long for me to be holy as a reflection of you to others. Teach me how to live a life of holiness. Alleluia. Glory in the highest. Amen.

For Reflection

- Write a letter or prayer to God thanking him for being your eternal Father.
- Write a prayer thanking God for the gift of grace.

DAY 28

TRANSFORMATION

Bible Reading: 2 Corinthians 3:18

And we, who with unveiled faces all reflect the Lord's glory, are being transformed into his likeness with ever-increasing glory, which comes from the Lord, who is the Spirit.

Oh, what a promise! As believers, we can be transformed to reflect Christ during this earthly life. We can have continual opportunities to surrender to the work of the Holy Spirit who provides us with power to display the fruit of the Holy Spirit: love, joy, peace, patience, kindness, goodness, faithfulness, gentleness, and self-control. We can be set free from unhealthy habits and call upon our Heavenly Father to replace these with new healthy behaviors that bring glory to Him.

Prayer Response

Dear Father,

    I call upon you to be the transformer of my life. I long to bring you glory in my relationships and lifestyle. Alleluia. Glory in the highest. Amen.

For Reflection

- Which fruit of the spirit is easiest for you to display? Which is most difficult?
- Spend time in prayer asking God for His help in displaying one or more of the fruits.

DAY 29

PROTECTION

Bible Reading: Ephesians 6:10,13

Finally, be strong in the Lord and in his mighty power. Therefore put on the full armor of God, so that when the day of evil comes, you may be able to stand your ground, and after you have done everything, to stand.

Poem

You gird us with your Word,
To protect us from evil thoughts and ways.

You give us your Spirit,
To guide us in our times of uncertainty.

You call us to pray,
When our heart is heavy for the burdens of other believers

You tell us to claim your truth,

When the evil one sends us lies to confuse and hurt us.

You guide us to hold onto your strength,
When we feel weak and inadequate.

You instruct us to be alert,
And take time to help fellow believers.

Prayer Response:

Father,

Thank you that you are a faithful and loving God who provides protection from evil and supplies what we need. May I be obedient to the guidance you provide. Alleluia. Amen.

For Reflection

- In what areas of your life do you desire God's protection?
- How has God already been faithful to provide protection?

DAY 30

PROMISES FOR ETERNITY

Bible Reading: Isaiah 40:8

The grass withers and the flowers fall, but the word of our God stands forever.

These encouraging words remind us of what is eternal and what is only temporary and will soon pass away. We can hold fast to promises found in Scripture which will remain with us into eternity. May we not become enticed to hold on to the things which this earthly world offers our eyes. Rather, let us open our mind and heart to God's Word. The same Word that can guide and comfort us now and throughout eternity.

Prayer Response

Father,

Thank you that I can trust in the promises of your Word both today and for eternity. When circumstances arise which cause me great fear and even hardship, your Word stands true. Alleluia. Glory in the highest. Amen.

For Reflection

- List any distractions which lead you away from spending time in God's Word (TV, social networking, WEB surfing or games, other).
- Describe your plan for spending daily time in God's Word.

NEXT STEPS

Here are some additional contemplative devotional books that you may want to read as you continue your devotional time.

God Calling by Anonymous
Jesus Calling by Sarah Young
My Utmost for His Highest by Oswald Chambers

My hope and prayer is that by reading this devotional book a desire is stirred to expand your time spent with the Lord each day.

CLOSING

The encouraging words I want to leave with you are found in Joshua 1:5,
"As I was with Moses, so I will be with you; I will never leave you nor forsake you."

NOTES

CPSIA information can be obtained at www.ICGtesting.com
Printed in the USA
BVOW010923100113

310216BV00001BA/1/P